In His Own Words

IN
HIS OWN
WORDS

Inspirational Reflections on the Life & Wisdom of
BILLY GRAHAM

JERRY B. JENKINS

TYNDALE
MOMENTUM®

The nonfiction imprint of
Tyndale House Publishers, Inc.

Visit Tyndale online at www.tyndale.com.

Visit Tyndale Momentum online at www.tyndalemomentum.com.

Visit Jerry B. Jenkins at www.JerryJenkins.com.

TYNDALE, Tyndale Momentum, and Tyndale's quill logo are registered trademarks of Tyndale House Publishers, Inc. The Tyndale Momentum logo is a trademark of Tyndale House Publishers, Inc. Tyndale Momentum is the nonfiction imprint of Tyndale House Publishers, Inc., Carol Stream, Illinois.

In His Own Words: Inspirational Reflections on the Life and Wisdom of Billy Graham

Designed by Jennifer Ghionzoli

Published in association with The Bindery Agency, www.TheBinderyAgency.com.

All Scripture quotations, unless otherwise indicated, are taken from the New King James Version,® copyright © 1982 by Thomas Nelson, Inc. Used by permission. All rights reserved.

Scripture quotations marked ESV are taken from *The Holy Bible*, English Standard Version® (ESV®), copyright © 2001 by Crossway, a publishing ministry of Good News Publishers. Used by permission. All rights reserved.

Scripture quotations marked KJV are taken from the *Holy Bible*, King James Version.

Scripture quotations marked NIV are taken from the Holy Bible, *New International Version*,® *NIV.*® Copyright © 1973, 1978, 1984, 2011 by Biblica, Inc.® Used by permission. All rights reserved worldwide.

Scripture quotations marked NLT are taken from the *Holy Bible*, New Living Translation, copyright © 1996, 2004, 2015 by Tyndale House Foundation. Used by permission of Tyndale House Publishers, Inc., Carol Stream, Illinois 60188. All rights reserved.

For information about special discounts for bulk purchases, please contact Tyndale House Publishers at csresponse@tyndale.com, or call 1-800-323-9400.

Library of Congress Cataloging-in-Publication Data

Names: Jenkins, Jerry B., author.
Title: In his own words : inspirational reflections on the life and wisdom of Billy Graham / Jerry B. Jenkins.
Description: Carol Stream, Illinois : Tyndale House Publishers, Inc., 2018. | Includes bibliographical references.
Identifiers: LCCN 2018022137 | ISBN 9781496436436 (hc : alk. paper)
Subjects: LCSH: Graham, Billy, 1918-2018.
Classification: LCC BV3785.G69 J46 2018 | DDC 269/.2092—dc23 LC record available at https://lccn.loc.gov/2018022137

Printed in the United States of America

24   23   22   21   20   19   18
7   6   5   4   3   2   1

TO STEPHANIE WILLS

◆

Blessed is she who believed,
for there will be a fulfillment of those things
which were told her from the Lord.

LUKE 1:45

And I, brethren, when I came to you, did not come with excellence of speech or of wisdom declaring to you the testimony of God. For I determined not to know anything among you except Jesus Christ and Him crucified.

THE APOSTLE PAUL IN I CORINTHIANS 2:1-2

Contents

The Paradox of Humility

The single most striking character trait attributed to Billy Graham—his humility—made him so instantly attractive that it warred against his very nature. The truly humble shun the spotlight, abhor attention, and labor to shift the focus elsewhere. In Mr. Graham's case, he pointed to Jesus.

Yet his particular modesty proved so magnetic, it made him a celebrity—the label he hated most. The cliché about one's presence lighting up a room could have been written for him. Everyone from waitstaff to heads of state were drawn to him, and he made Gallup's annual list of the world's most admired people sixty-one times—more than any other man or woman.

Billy Graham never wavered from his sole message: salvation by grace through faith in the work of Christ on the cross. Yet he once lamented to me that "nine of ten people on the street would tell you my message was the opposite. They believe I urged them to live right, to do more, to work harder, to go to church, to pray, to read their Bibles—all wonderful things. But those will not save you. The Bible says we're saved by grace through faith and 'not of yourselves; it is the gift of God, not of works, lest anyone should boast'" (Ephesians 2:8-9).

His statistics stagger the imagination. The most famous evangelist since the apostle Paul, Mr. Graham spoke live to more than 215 million people in 185 countries over the course of more than 60 years. Yet he was never about numbers. When the press raised the subject, he'd say, "It's not how many people can I get into the stadium, but how many people can I get the word out to." About 3 million people indicated that they came to faith in Christ at one of his crusades.

A confidant and spiritual adviser to twelve US presidents, Mr. Graham was an early leader in civil rights, integrating his Southern meetings as early as 1953. An innovator in the use of media, Graham used radio, television, films, books, and a syndicated newspaper column to reach an audience estimated at nearly 3 billion people. He founded the Billy Graham Evangelistic Association in 1950 with the aim of using every means of modern communication to spread the Gospel.

Despite the staggering reach of his message, when Mr. Graham was asked how he would want his obituary to read, he said simply, "That I loved the Lord with all my mind and soul and spirit." And as for his epitaph? "Preacher."

How gratifying to know that despite his passing, there is no epitaph on Mr. Graham's worldwide ministry and influence. Under the leadership of his son Franklin, the work of the Billy Graham Evangelistic Association continues. The organization scheduled twenty-four Gospel preaching events in ten countries in 2018 alone. BGEA also maintains a twenty-four-hour-a-day worldwide Internet presence. The Billy Graham Library in Charlotte, North Carolina, ministers to thousands of visitors annually. The Billy Graham Training Center at The Cove in Asheville, North Carolina, hosts Bible conferences year-round. And the BGEA's Rapid Response Team, created in the aftermath of 9/11, has responded to more than 350 crises in twenty countries.

In every endeavor, Billy Graham's goal was to point others to Christ—and that was true even when writing his autobiography. In the early 1990s, I enjoyed the unspeakable privilege of assisting Mr. Graham with that book, *Just As I Am*. For thirteen months I traveled to and from his home on Black Mountain in Montreat, North Carolina. I spent hours interviewing him for the autobiography, but we also spent a great deal of time in informal conversation, both at his house as well as on the road.

I took careful notes, with his permission. For this book, I not only combed through Mr. Graham's published books, articles, and interviews, but I also perused the Billy Graham Evangelistic Association website and referred to our conversations.

I'll never forget those precious hours with him. My wife says that whenever I returned from Montreat, I seemed to be floating two feet off the ground.

I found Billy Graham the same behind closed doors as he appeared in public. Humble. Single-minded. A true man of God.

Jerry B. Jenkins
BLACK FOREST, COLORADO

PART ONE

HIS SINGULAR MESSAGE

Evangelism
is the Gospel,
the Good News,
presented to all.

BILLY GRAHAM

Billy Graham's weakness, critics said, was the simplicity of his message. Yet those who benefited from it—particularly those who came to faith because of it—knew it was his greatest strength.

"I preach Christ and Him crucified," Mr. Graham would say. And that was true whether he was speaking to the largest crowd in his history—1.1 million in Seoul, South Korea, in 1973—or to a busboy at a suburban Chicago eatery decades later. Regardless of the venue or the audience, Billy Graham shared the Gospel.

Before great stadium crowds, he often began his message with local references, proclaiming the host city "the gateway to the magnificent continent of Asia" or "America's beautiful Eastern seaboard." Then he moved directly into the current world scene, painting a word picture of the geopolitical chaos and turmoil, acknowledging the fear that gripped the nations. But soon he zeroed in on the deepest needs of the human heart.

In minutes, Mr. Graham—piercing voice booming—moved from the global to the personal. His distinctive, authoritative, passionate preaching targeted each listener's loneliness, fear, uncertainty over the future, and feeling of emptiness. And his message was always the same. He eschewed esoteric doctrine and sidestepped specific moral, especially religious, controversy. Listeners around the world said they felt he was speaking directly to them, spotlighting their most private needs.

Billy Graham's most common phrases were "The Bible says . . ." and "Jesus is the answer!"

And while his volume and tone varied for the more intimate mediums of radio and television, or during one-on-one conversations, he always moved quickly to his singular message. He explained it this way:

> First, you must recognize what God did: that He loved you so much, He gave His Son to die on the cross.
>
> Second, you must repent of your sins.
>
> Third, you must receive Jesus Christ as Savior and Lord. This means you cease trying to save yourself and trust Him completely, without reservation.
>
> Fourth, you must confess Christ publicly as a sign that you have been converted. It is extremely important that you tell someone else about it as soon as possible.[*]

---

[*] Adapted from Billy Graham, *How to Be Born Again* (Waco, TX: Word, 1977), 168.

◆

*If you confess with your mouth the Lord Jesus and
believe in your heart that God has raised Him
from the dead, you will be saved. For with the
heart one believes unto righteousness, and with
the mouth confession is made unto salvation.*

ROMANS 10:9-10

God proved His love
on the cross. When Christ
hung, and bled, and died,
it was God saying to
the world, "I love you."

BILLY GRAHAM

One of the most iconic photographic images from Billy Graham's crusades depicts him—following his message and the invitation—standing with his head bowed, chin resting on folded hands. Asked what went through his mind at those moments, as thousands streamed forward to make their decisions for Christ, he said he was praying that God would move mightily in the hearts of those who longed for Him but feared making the commitment. "I prayed He would give them the courage. And I thanked Him for the privilege of playing a role in someone's salvation."

But, Mr. Graham said, at the same time he was overwhelmed by a sense of fatigue, as if every physical reserve had been drained from his body. "I knew the power to preach the Gospel was not my own, that every conversion was the work of the Holy Spirit." And yet he was soaked with sweat, having given his all to plead, cajole, and persuade people to listen to the urgings of the Spirit.

The evangelist deflected the question of why his ministry seemed uniquely successful among similar ministries. Analysts said there were better preachers, better evangelists, better theologians, smarter—or at least more educated—clerics, so why him? Outsiders speculated he was the best showman, a savvier promoter. In truth, he was embarrassed that his name was used so prominently in advertising a crusade, yet he knew his very visibility drew the curious.

"The first question I plan to ask the Lord when I get to Heaven is 'Why me?'" he said. "I still see myself as a Southern boy from a dairy farm. But I answered a call to preach, and God has done all the rest."

◆

God so loved the world that He gave His only begotten Son, that whoever believes in Him should not perish but have everlasting life. For God did not send His Son into the world to condemn the world, but that the world through Him might be saved.

JOHN 3:16-17

I enjoy watching
a runner cross home plate,
but nothing thrills me
more than seeing the Holy
Spirit at work in hearts as
the Gospel is carried into
stadiums, across the airwaves,
and around the world.

Growing up on the family farm outside Charlotte, North Carolina, Billy Graham was a hyperactive kid who loved playing baseball. His hero was Babe Ruth of the New York Yankees, and Billy dreamt of one day playing at Yankee Stadium and at Chicago's Wrigley Field. When the Babe barnstormed around the country during Billy's first year of high school, his team showed up for an exhibition game in Charlotte. Billy and his friends sat in the front row. Somehow his dad finagled a handshake between him and the Babe, and Graham says he didn't wash his hands for three days.

In high school, Billy was a reserve first baseman and realized he would never make the big leagues. He batted left-handed, like the Babe, but had to train himself to keep his left hand on top. (As an adult he played golf right-handed but often played with his left hand on top of the club.)

The evangelist was fascinated by how rabid sports fans could become. He watched occasional games on television when he had time, and baseball remained his favorite sport. As much as he enjoyed getting wrapped up in a game that wasn't decided until the last inning, he said he never got carried away with it as many die-hard fans did.

"I suppose it wouldn't have been appropriate to jump and clap and cheer at an evangelistic crusade—because most of us were raised that that was something you didn't do in church or at any sort of religious gathering. But that's where I rejoiced, at least inwardly. That's the kind of stadium activity that thrilled me."

◆

Go therefore and make disciples of all the nations, baptizing them in the name of the Father and of the Son and of the Holy Spirit, teaching them to observe all things that I have commanded you.

MATTHEW 28:19-20

I've wept as I've gone
from city to city and
I've seen how far people
have wandered from God.

BILLY GRAHAM

Although Billy Graham's passion to see people come to Christ was evident throughout his ministry, as a young man he had not wanted to become a pastor, a preacher, or an evangelist. In fact, despite studying at a small Bible college in Florida, he at first resisted the calling he felt God placing on his heart. But as he began learning and growing as a preacher, speaking here and there, many listeners responded by becoming believers in Christ. His teachers and classmates encouraged him, telling Graham they believed the ministry was right for him. Once he sensed the Holy Spirit affirming this as well, he struggled.

Billy felt a passion for souls, as the great nineteenth-century evangelist D. L. Moody described his own calling, but did he want to make a life of preaching? Every night for weeks he agonized over this on walks around a deserted golf course. In his autobiography, *Just As I Am*, Mr. Graham recalled feeling an "inner, irresistible urge" to submit to God one night. Falling to his knees and then flat on the ground, he cried, "O God, if You want me to serve You, I will."

But now that Billy had obeyed and become eager to preach, opportunities seemed to dry up. The school year ended, and most students left for the summer.

He stayed on to do odd jobs, hoping to be invited to preach somewhere. A week went by, and nothing. He even applied at a few local churches, but they either had no openings or weren't interested in a novice.

Finally, one day Billy was cutting grass on campus when he saw a man he recognized as the director of the West Tampa Gospel Mission. This man often asked students to assist him, but he had never asked Graham. Billy wondered if he ever would and had, by now, begun questioning the legitimacy of his own call to ministry. He dropped to his knees behind a bush and prayed that God would allow him to preach at the man's mission the following day.

When he looked up, the man came directly to him, telling Billy his speaker for the next day had canceled and asking if he would fill in.

Billy so enjoyed preaching to the small group of young men at the mission that he asked the director if he could also preach on the streets. He preached seven sermons that same day, mostly in front of saloons, and did the same every weekend for the next two years. Once he stopped resisting God's call on his life, he was off and running as a preacher.

◆

Christ did not send me to baptize, but to preach the gospel, not with wisdom of words, lest the cross of Christ should be made of no effect.

For the message of the cross is foolishness to those who are perishing, but to us who are being saved it is the power of God.

1 CORINTHIANS 1:17-18

The Gospel has
never changed.

I have never changed
my message. I preach
the Bible, and I preach
it with authority.

BILLY GRAHAM

The most pivotal moment in Billy Graham's spiritual life—aside from his own conversion at age sixteen—came late in the summer of 1949, prior to what was to become his most ambitious citywide evangelistic effort to date. Graham and his team had scheduled a three-week tent crusade to begin the last week of September in Los Angeles.

Mr. Graham had been invited to speak at the annual College Briefing Conference at Forest Home, a meeting center near LA. He wrote in *Just As I Am* that he arrived conflicted over his view of Scripture. He had never doubted his salvation, the Gospel, or the truths of Christ. But a former colleague and fellow evangelist chided Graham that he had an old-fashioned view of the Bible. Chuck Templeton, who had left the pastorate and evangelistic preaching to get an advanced degree, believed Billy was out of step with the times. Templeton challenged him to study more and learn that no one took the Bible seriously any longer.

Graham wondered whether he had been naive to believe the Bible was inerrant. If he couldn't state categorically that he believed the Bible was exactly what it claimed to be, he would have to stop preaching. During the days of the conference, Mr. Graham was encouraged in his faith. But during the evenings, he continued to suffer in prayer over his view of Scripture.

One evening alone in his room, Billy read as many verses as he could find that included "thus saith the Lord." But finally in frustration he stormed out into the night for a walk in the woods. He set his open Bible on a tree stump in the darkness, warring within himself whether he could trust it as the Word of God. He dropped to his knees, confessing that he didn't understand everything and couldn't reconcile the seeming contradictions intellectuals pointed out. Philosophical, scientific, and psychological questions his friend Templeton had raised plagued him.

But finally, Billy Graham felt in his heart what he must do. "Father," he cried out. "I am going to accept this as Thy Word—by faith!"

A month later the Los Angeles crusade opened, but it didn't end in three weeks. Mr. Graham, preaching with an authority and confidence he had never known, saw thousands fill the tent every night and many come forward to receive Christ. The meetings continued for eight weeks and could have gone longer. For the next six decades, similar results were duplicated in cities all over the world.

◆

I [do not] count my life dear to myself,
so that I may finish my race with joy, and
the ministry which I received from the Lord Jesus,
to testify to the gospel of the grace of God.

ACTS 20:24

The Bible says today is the accepted time, today is the day of salvation.... But there will come a time when it will be too late.

BILLY GRAHAM

Billy Graham was widely criticized for his passion-ate altar calls at the end of each crusade message. Some felt he unfairly played on people's emotions, and others were concerned that those who responded might wrongly believe their souls were saved simply because they walked forward.

But according to former Moody Bible Institute president Michael Easley, that accusation is much older than Billy Graham. Apparently many leveled the same charge against nineteenth-century mass evangelist D. L. Moody. When Moody was criticized for his meth-ods, he reportedly responded, "I like my way of doing evangelism better than your way of not doing it."

Easley acknowledged that a person could wrongly assume that merely going forward was "equivalent to salvation." However, he pointed out that trained coun-selors were there to clarify the process of coming to faith and that, even then, the Graham organization was under no illusion that every person who came forward had been saved.

Mr. Graham said he always included an altar call because "it was the whole point. We were there to share the Gospel and to give men and women the opportunity to respond to it." He also cited D. L. Moody's reason for a sense of urgency. Moody once told a Chicago audience to think and pray about their decision to follow Christ and be prepared to act upon it the next Sunday. But that very night the Great Chicago Fire swept through the city, and Moody was forever haunted by the fear that some he'd sent home to ponder God's invitation might have been lost for eternity. Moody never again postponed an altar call.

And Billy Graham never preached without including one.

♦

Behold, now is the accepted time; behold,
now is the day of salvation.

2 CORINTHIANS 6:2

Almost everybody will listen to you when you tell your own story.

BILLY GRAHAM

Of those who complained they were rarely success-ful in witnessing to others, Billy Graham said they were likely going about it the wrong way. It's not effective, he said, when you simply tell people what they ought to do. "Rather, tell what's happened to you, how the Gospel and your relationship with Christ have changed your life. Then people are more likely to ask you to explain the plan of salvation."

Just before the 1949 Los Angeles tent crusade that would become the launching pad for Mr. Graham's decades-long international preaching ministry, he spoke to what was known as the Hollywood Christian Group in Beverly Hills. Many celebrities attended, including singer-songwriter Stuart Hamblen, host of the most popular daily radio broadcast on the West Coast. While his wife was a believer and his father a Methodist preacher in Texas, Hamblen had strayed from his upbringing and claimed no faith. But he joked that if he endorsed Mr. Graham's upcoming crusade, he could fill the tent every night.

Once the crusade started, Hamblen did have Mr. Graham on his show and surprised him by not only urging listeners to go hear Billy Graham preach but also by adding that he planned to attend too.

Three weeks later, when the crusade was scheduled to end, Billy and his team debated whether to extend the meetings because the crowds were growing. On the day of the last scheduled event, Mr. Graham was awakened at 4:30 in the morning by a call from Stuart Hamblen. In tears he told the evangelist he needed to see him right away. By the time Graham was dressed, Hamblen and his wife showed up at his hotel, and soon the singer had received Christ as his Savior.

The team decided to extend the meetings, and during the next week Hamblen gave his testimony over the air. His was only the first of many from other luminaries as well as common people. The crowds grew, and the three-week campaign eventually lasted eight weeks.

Hamblen soon wrote the song "It Is No Secret (What God Can Do)" and later the classic "This Ole House." He used every means possible to tell what Christ had done for him. And people listened.

◆

I am not ashamed of the gospel of Christ, for it is the power of God to salvation for everyone who believes.

ROMANS 1:16

I'm grateful for the opportunities God gave me to minister to people in high places; people in power have spiritual and personal needs like everyone else, and often they have no one to talk to.

BILLY GRAHAM

A national weekly news magazine writer, crafting a Billy Graham obituary years before he died (not unusual for famous people), suggested to a Graham confidant that Billy was an inveterate name-dropper.

"Oh, you mean because he often talks about having met heads of state and other famous people?"

"Exactly!"

"Knowing him, I believe he truly does not see himself in their category and can't believe he's been privileged to meet them."

The reporter pressed, "He mentions them so frequently."

The confidant said, "But have you noticed that he never breaks their confidences, nor does he say anything negative about them?"

Mr. Graham admitted the name-dropping label bothered him when it popped up in stories and profiles. "It's not true that I mention names to try to impress. It's just that I've lived so long and traveled so much that I've met a lot of people like that. They've become my friends, and I like to talk about my friends."

When the evangelist passed away in February 2018, many of his obituaries did play up the name-dropper theme. But most also noted that Graham was nearly as famous as any president, king, queen, crown prince, or prime minister he'd ever met.

"I always shared the Gospel with them and prayed with them," he said. "They were my friends."

◆

When they bring you to the synagogues and magistrates and authorities, do not worry about how or what you should answer, or what you should say. For the Holy Spirit will teach you in that very hour what you ought to say.

LUKE 12:11-12

PART TWO

CHRISTIAN LIVING

Be on guard against
a self-centered pride
that ultimately will destroy
you. Instead, see yourself
the way God sees you,
and humbly accept the
gifts He has given you.

BILLY GRAHAM

Early in the 1990s, an interviewer asked Mr. Graham, "How does it feel to be so popular that hundreds of thousands come to hear you preach in stadiums all over the world?"

The evangelist looked puzzled, as if he had genuinely never thought about that. Then while the two watched a black-and-white film highlighting his 1950s crusades, Graham wept quietly at the sight of 120,000 people packed into London's Wembley Stadium for the final night of his 1954 United Kingdom meetings. He had preached to a million and a half people in three months.

"That must have been so gratifying," the interviewer suggested.

Mr. Graham ignored the prompt and said, "Let's just pray and thank the Lord for what we just saw."

When Billy looked up from praying, the interviewer asked if he didn't at least appreciate how current crowds greeted him with warm applause.

He shook his head. "I smile, but I'd rather dig a hole and crawl into it."

"But they're just thanking you . . ."

"I know, but the Bible says God will not share His glory with another."

◆

I am the LORD; that is my name!
I will not give my glory to anyone else,
nor share my praise.

ISAIAH 42:8, NLT

The highest form of worship is the worship of unselfish Christian service. The greatest form of praise is the sound of consecrated feet seeking out the lost and helpless.

BILLY GRAHAM

At the peak of his popularity and recognizability in the early 1950s, Billy Graham dined in New York with a friend, who commented on all the media attention Graham and his crusades enjoyed. The evangelist had just returned from the massive three-month affair in London that had drawn record crowds.

"I'm scared I'm going to get the credit for what God is doing," Mr. Graham said. "And that's just not right."

More than fifty years later, after touring the Billy Graham Library just before its 2007 opening, Graham was asked his impressions of it. After extolling the quality of many of the exhibits, particularly the area devoted to his wife, Ruth, Mr. Graham confessed to one misgiving. "Too much Billy, not enough Jesus." Staff had to assure him that every display was designed to focus visitors on Graham's heart's message—the Gospel of Christ.

Mr. Graham's reservations about his own visibility carried over to his autobiography, *Just As I Am*, and led to many crises of doubt over whether he should finish it. It seemed as if every month he seriously considered abandoning the project. His aides had to encourage him to stay with it. One told him, "When people are exposed to you, they immediately see what you're all about. So let them get to know you in this book and they'll know all you care about is that they get to know Jesus."

♦

He must increase, but I must decrease. He who comes from above is above all; he who is of the earth is earthly and speaks of the earth. He who comes from heaven is above all. And what He has seen and heard, that He testifies.

JOHN 3:30-32

The Bible tells us to
pray without ceasing and
to search the Scriptures,
and I do that.

BILLY GRAHAM

An interviewer visiting Mr. Graham in his office asked if he really prayed without ceasing.

He said, "I do, and I have every waking moment since I received Christ at age sixteen. I pray while I'm speaking, whether preaching or just conversing. I'm praying right now as I'm talking to you that everything I say will glorify Christ."

Worried Billy Graham's example set the bar too high for the average believer, the interviewer asked, "What form does your searching the Scriptures take?"

Mr. Graham said, "Wherever I am in the world—in someone's home, my home, a hotel room, here in my office, anywhere—I leave my Bible open where I'll notice it during the day. Every time I see it, I stop and read a verse or two, or a chapter or two, or for an hour or two. And this is not for sermon preparation; it's just for my own spiritual nourishment."

Now the interviewer felt he was getting somewhere. Everyone wants a daily devotional life, even if they can't literally pray without ceasing. "How do you get back into it if you miss a day or two?"

The evangelist cocked his head and squinted. "I don't think I've ever done that."

"You never miss?"

"No, I said it's nourishment for my spiritual life, and I don't want to miss a meal."

Over Mr. Graham's shoulder, on the corner of his desk, lay his open Bible, just as he said.

◆

Pray without ceasing.

1 THESSALONIANS 5:17

◆

This Book of the Law shall not depart from your mouth, but you shall meditate in it day and night, that you may observe to do according to all that is written in it.

JOSHUA 1:8

Everyone must kneel at the cross and acknowledge that he needs the grace of God. No one can come proudly to Christ.

BILLY GRAHAM

During an interview in his modest office in Montreat, North Carolina, Mr. Graham sat low in a dilapidated easy chair and talked about the number of times he had failed the Lord. "It makes me feel this low," he said, reaching to place his palm flat on the floor.

That simple gesture made the interviewer believe that every word the man had spoken was true. This was not a show, not an act. "Sold out to Christ" defined who he was at his core.

Ruth Graham's first impression of her eventual husband was that he "wanted to please God more than any man I'd ever met." And the way he prayed proved to her that he had an unusually intimate relationship with God—"as if he knew who he was talking to."

Despite ranking among the most admired—and recognizable—people in the world for decades, Billy Graham exuded such modesty that he convinced strangers they were more important than he was. He seemed as happy to meet and talk with a train porter or a flight attendant as with a head of state. Even detractors who met with him went away with changed attitudes. They still might not have agreed with him, but they could no longer dislike him or continue to question his motives.

Quoting 1 Corinthians 9:22, Mr. Graham explained, "I want to say with the apostle Paul, 'to the weak I became as weak, that I might win the weak. I have become all things to all men, that I might by all means save some.'"

◆

By grace you have been saved through faith,
and that not of yourselves; it is the gift of God,
not of works, lest anyone should boast.

EPHESIANS 2:8-9

God loves you,
and He *wants* you
to know His will.
Seek it … discover it
… and then do it.
His way is always best.

BILLY GRAHAM

At home while recovering from hip surgery, Mr. Graham had to have an injection. His doctor said, "Billy, I have to give you this directly into the pelvic bone, and it's going to be terribly painful. I recommend you try to imagine yourself somewhere else, maybe in some Shangri-la."

Mr. Graham said, "No, there's nowhere I'd rather be than right here right now."

"Why would you say that? I told you, this is *really* going to hurt."

"Because I always want to be in the center of God's will," Mr. Graham said. "If this is where He has me today, this is where I want to be."

◆

I will instruct you and teach you
in the way you should go;
I will guide you with My eye.

PSALM 32:8

I read five Psalms
every day to learn how
to get along with God.
Then I read a chapter
of Proverbs every day
to learn how to get along
with my fellow man.

BILLY GRAHAM

Early in his public ministry, Billy Graham was blindsided and injured by letters from critics who blasted him for everything from the churches represented on crusade-planning committees to whom he invited to sit on the platform at these events. He knew his own heart, he said, and sincerely had one aim: to preach the Gospel and see men and women come to saving faith. How was it possible, he wondered, that people who may have disagreed with some aspect of his approach could jump to such wild conclusions about his motives?

"I 'bout drove Ruth crazy back then, reading these horrible letters charging me with everything from blasphemy to heresy and even knowingly sending people to Hell. I'd read them over and over and ask her if she could believe it. What she couldn't believe, she said, was that I wasted my time on them. She'd tell me people would think what they wanted to think, and no answer from me would make a difference. She wanted me to stick to doing what I knew was right and let the naysayers be."

But at the time, Billy Graham's temperament did not allow him to do that. Whenever he received such a letter, he would make notes, deconstructing every disparaging line and trying to craft the perfect response. Then he would dictate a long, thoughtful answer he just knew would change minds and win arguments. He suggested to many that he and they could disagree about whom he might have on the platform, but couldn't they agree that he never let that soften his message? He always preached Christ, and if some of his guests were liberals or had a less reverent view of Scripture, perhaps they were hearing the clear Gospel for the first time.

But Ruth was right. All the time he invested in trying to persuade critics was wasted. His replies merely triggered long-distance debates, and Mr. Graham spent more time defending himself than preparing sermons. He prayed about it, consulted more seasoned clergy, and even discussed it with his clerical staff. Finally, he felt the Lord impress upon him an answer from Proverbs 15:1-2: "A soft answer turns away wrath, but a harsh word stirs up anger. The tongue of the wise uses knowledge rightly, but the mouth of fools pours forth foolishness."

The next time, and every time thereafter, that Graham was assaulted by a hateful, accusatory letter, he directed that this reply be sent:

Dear [Name]:

Thank you for caring enough to be so forthright in your letter. I trust I can count on you to pray for me as I continue to try to serve the Lord.

Sincerely in Christ,
Billy Graham

That didn't end the criticism, but it did result in new, wholly different responses. Sure, he said, some fired back asking if he was too daft to understand what they'd written the first time. But now, more often than not, many wrote back apologizing for their tone and assuring him that they would indeed pray for him.

◆

If it is possible, as much as depends on you,
live peaceably with all men.
ROMANS 12:18

I've found Christian people more than generous in understanding my faults. . . . I am an erring, fallible disciple of our Lord Jesus Christ and am subject to all the temptations, human frailties, and errors of other disciples of the Lord.

BILLY GRAHAM

A 1950 audience with Harry Truman—Billy Graham's first meeting with a president—resulted in what he considered his first major public gaffe. He recounted it so many times throughout the rest of his life that Ruth said she was tired of hearing it. "It's over, you learned from it. Move on."

After congressmen helped Graham secure a meeting with the president in Washington in June 1950, he asked three close associates to go with him. They paired white buck shoes—which they'd seen Truman wearing in a photo—with their summer suits for the occasion.

They arrived at the White House and met first with the president's secretary, who told them they would spend exactly twenty minutes with President Truman. They were then ushered into the Oval Office. Mr. Graham later recalled that the president's bemused expression made them wonder if he thought a group of entertainers had stopped by for a chat.

As their meeting drew to a close, the president agreed to Graham's suggestion that they end in prayer. After leaving the White House, Graham and his associates were surrounded by reporters and photographers. When asked about their conversation with the president, Billy Graham told them everything he could remember. A photographer asked the group to kneel on the lawn and reenact the prayer Graham had prayed in the Oval Office. The other journalists quickly expressed their approval.

Though Mr. Graham refused to divulge the words of that prayer, he agreed to publicly thank God for the opportunity to meet with Mr. Truman. A photographer took a picture of the four men, each on one knee with his head bowed as Mr. Graham led a prayer of thanksgiving.

Within a few days, Mr. Graham realized he'd made a mistake and offended the president by quoting him without prior authorization. In fact, a prominent newspaper columnist reported that he was now considered a persona non grata by the administration.

As painful as that experience was, it may have prevented Billy Graham future humiliation. As he recalled in *Just As I Am*: "I vowed to myself it would never happen again if I ever was given access to a person of rank or influence."

◆

If we confess our sins, He is faithful and just to forgive us our sins and to cleanse us from all unrighteousness.

1 JOHN 1:9

If I had it all to do
over again, I'd study more
and preach less.

BILLY GRAHAM

Billy Graham often said that not studying enough was one of his great regrets. He felt pressured into speaking to local groups when he should have been preparing for what he knew was his primary calling. He quoted pastor and theologian Dr. Donald Grey Barnhouse that if he knew the Lord was coming in three years he would "spend two of them studying and one preaching."

Another of his regrets, Graham said, was that he "did not spend enough time with my family when they were growing up. You cannot recapture those years." Until his death, he warned younger preachers not to follow that example. His carefully documented itinerary through the decades showed him out of the country for weeks, then home for one day before jetting to Dallas or New York or Chicago, home another day, and off again. That pattern continued year after year, as did his journal entries expressing regret over it and pledging to do better. "But I never did," he said sadly.

Later in his ministry, when Ruth was seriously injured in a fall at the home of one of their daughters, Mr. Graham had to be persuaded to leave a crusade several hundred miles away to visit her in the hospital. Once home, his daughters pleaded with him to let someone else finish preaching the crusade so he could stay with Ruth, but he hurried back the same day.

"I had the right motives," he recounted, "at least in my own mind. It was a fact that the crowds were smaller when I was not there. I didn't insist on preaching due to ego, but because I felt a responsibility. I was wrong, and my place was at home. My daughters have always been loving and gracious to me, but I don't believe they ever forgave me for that. At least they never forgot it. Ruth assured me she did, but I wouldn't let her. I apologized so many times, she said I bordered on insulting her ability to forgive and forget."

♦

Study to shew thyself approved unto God,
a workman that needeth not to be ashamed,
rightly dividing the word of truth.

2 TIMOTHY 2:15, KJV

PART THREE

HUMOR

God's strength is
made perfect in weakness.
The weaker I became,
the more powerful became
the preaching.

BILLY GRAHAM

One morning at a hotel barbershop in Fort Lauderdale, Florida, Mr. Graham was getting a haircut when a manicurist struck up a conversation with him, asking, "So what do you do?"

In his inimitable accent, Mr. Graham said, "I'm a preachah."

She said, "Oh, I don't care that much for preachers. Except Billy Graham—I like him."

He said, "You like Billy Graham, do you?"

She nodded. "I really learn from him."

"Well, thank you. I am Billy Graham."

She frowned. "Oh, you don't even look like him!"

The barber caught her eye and mouthed, "It's really him."

She said, "Oh, my God!"

And Mr. Graham said, "No, but I work for Him."

◆

Know that the LORD, He is God;
It is He who has made us, and not we ourselves;
We are His people and the sheep of His pasture.

PSALM 100:3

Romance should last
a lifetime, and Ruth's
and mine did.

BILLY GRAHAM

As the evangelist was being interviewed for his autobiography, Ruth kept correcting him from another room. "That wasn't 1951, Bill," she'd say. "That was 1950. And it wasn't Bev, it was Cliff. And it wasn't Boston, it was New York."

Mr. Graham rolled his eyes. "Ruth," he said, "I wish you'd let me handle my own memoirs."

"Well, I would," she called back, "but they're starting to sound like your forgetoirs!"

Ruth recounted to an interviewer that their eldest daughter, Gigi, overheard her father tell her (Ruth) before he left for India once in the 1950s that he wanted no more than two fireplaces in the new home Ruth was having built for them. When he returned, he found five fireplaces and began to scold her. "Oh," Ruth interrupted, "I thought you said no *fewer* than two."

Ruth said Gigi pulled her aside. "You know Daddy said no more than two!"

"Gigi," Ruth told her, "there comes a time to stop submitting and start outwitting."

Ruth Graham adored her husband. Once when he said something about the aging man who looked back at him from the mirror every morning, she told a visitor, "I love every well-earned line in that face. He's as handsome to me now as he was the day I met him."

But she could also be humorously honest with him and about him. She noted that if two people agree on everything, "one of them is unnecessary." Asked whether she had ever considered divorce, she said, "Never. Murder occasionally, but never divorce."

As they aged, Ruth became confined to a wheelchair or her bed. Mr. Graham said they found themselves more in love than they'd ever been. "Eventually she was in so much pain I could not even touch her. I would just sit by her bed, and we would look at each other, sometimes for hours. We continued our lifetime love affair with our eyes."

In later years, when Mr. Graham was himself homebound with many infirmities, he said he had come to love every fireplace in that house.

◆

Who can find a virtuous wife?
For her worth is far above rubies.
The heart of her husband safely trusts her;
So he will have no lack of gain.
She does him good and not evil
All the days of her life.

PROVERBS 31:10-12

I am not a great preacher,
and I don't claim to be. …
I'm an ordinary preacher,
just communicating the
Gospel in the best way
I know how.

BILLY GRAHAM

As lead editor of *Christianity Today* magazine, Dr. V. Gilbert Beers and his wife, Arlie, once traveled to England with Billy (founder of the magazine) and Ruth Graham to experience one of his crusades. One day as the four of them drove through the countryside, they stopped for a roadside picnic. When they were settled on the grass, Mr. Graham said, "Gil, why don't you say the blessing and then offer a devotion?"

Beers said he had never been more scared in his life. Maybe it was common for Billy Graham to "offer a devotion" off the top of his head, but Gil couldn't imagine ever being asked to do that in front of the greatest preacher in the world.

A pastor in Boston once noticed Mr. Graham sitting among his congregation and said, "Trying to preach a sermon with Billy Graham in the pew is like trying to pilot a ship with Noah onboard!"

Billy Graham sincerely believed he was an ordinary preacher, and he had a long list of pastors he loved to listen to. "They weren't just every bit as good as I was, they were far better. I never understood why the Lord blessed me so, but I do believe I was obedient. I wasn't led to be eloquent or scholarly. I knew I was to preach the Gospel, plain and simple. That's what people have always been hungry for."

The truth, however, was that while Graham was often criticized for the simplicity of his message, clearly he was among the most gifted speakers ever. He exuded warmth and charisma, and he could be as dramatic or as low-key as he chose. His accent was distinctive and intriguing, and in his prime his voice was powerful and piercing, rising for just the right emphasis at the most crucial points. Listeners often said they were drawn to his passion and authoritative tone. One said, "It was clear he believed God had given him his message, and he delivered it with that full confidence."

◆

Preach the word! Be ready in season and out of season. Convince, rebuke, exhort, with all longsuffering and teaching.

2 TIMOTHY 4:2

The Bible tells us to sing, not necessarily to sing well. And that's a good thing for me.

BILLY GRAHAM

A Sunday morning visitor to the Graham home tells the story of Billy inviting him to church. "He's so beloved that even at his own nearby church, people tended to flock to him. He knew it caused disruption, so he suggested we go a few minutes late and slip unnoticed into the back."

The visitor says that when they arrived, the congregation was standing and singing a hymn. "We found room in a pew near the back. All I could think was what an incredible privilege this was—to stand next to Billy Graham and share a hymnal! I was so moved, I couldn't sing."

Mr. Graham always insisted he couldn't carry a tune. In fact, though he occasionally "sang" with George Beverly Shea or Cliff Barrows, in reality he only shouted "No!" to their musical question, "Hide it under a bushel?"

That morning the evangelist's companion learned the truth. Not only could Graham not carry a tune, he seemed to have only one note, and it didn't match anything on the musical scale. "The irony was not lost on me. I had a story for the rest of my life. I was too emotional to sing, and Mr. Graham only growled the words with no semblance of the melody. I was sharing a hymnal with the most famous Christian in the world, but neither of us was singing."

♦

Make a joyful noise unto the LORD, all the earth:
make a loud noise, and rejoice, and sing praise.

PSALM 98:4, KJV

The only time my prayers are never answered is on the golf course.

BILLY GRAHAM

When Gerald Ford was president of the United States, he invited Billy Graham to play golf in a foursome that included the legend Jack Nicklaus and another leading pro. An avid player—in fact, golf was one of his only pastimes—Graham very much looked forward to the opportunity. Occasionally shooting in the seventies, he was a much better player than the president. Though he was honored to play with Ford, Billy was most excited about getting a close look at the best player in history up to that time—Nicklaus—as well as seeing what he could learn from the other pro.

The day before the outing, a fellow Christian on the PGA tour confided to Mr. Graham that the second pro in his foursome didn't sound happy about the prospect of playing with the evangelist. He said he just knew Graham would be spouting Bible verses and acting holier than thou. While Billy was always eager to share his faith, he prayed through his strategy and felt led to take an entirely different approach the next day.

"I didn't even bring up the subject," he recalled. "I didn't pray, didn't mention the Lord, just concentrated on enjoying the round and being as friendly and encouraging as I could be." When it was over, the result was as predicted. (Nicklaus shot the lowest score, followed by the other pro who was far off his usual game, then Graham, and finally the president.) The four shook hands and went their separate ways.

Graham was stunned to hear from his friend that the pro in question had stormed off the course and onto a practice range, swearing about his horrible time with the foursome. Someone asked him if things had gone the way he expected, with Mr. Graham shoving religion down his throat. "No," the pro finally admitted. "I kept waiting for it, but he was perfectly fine. I shot a horrible round though."

◆

I have fought a good fight,
I have finished my course.

2 TIMOTHY 4:7, KJV

PART FOUR

AGING AND DEATH

Old is authentic.
Old is genuine.
Old is valuable.

BILLY GRAHAM

Billy Graham was especially grateful for Ruth's upbringing. She grew up in China where her parents were medical missionaries. Her father, L. Nelson Bell, became one of Billy's most trusted mentors and confidants.

From the Chinese, Ruth learned to greatly respect her elders. It was common for her to quote Leviticus 19:32: "Stand up in the presence of the aged, show respect for the elderly" (NIV).

Mr. Graham felt that Western society largely abandoned that respect during the latter part of the twentieth century. "We seem to have the opposite view today," he said. "We value youth, and we tend to be afraid of getting older. Think of the billions we spend on cosmetics and medicines that claim they'll make us younger!" Yet he pointed out that some of our best years may lie ahead of us.

The evangelist counseled us to see ourselves as God sees us. When we do, we can entrust ourselves to God. No matter our age, God's children "are just as valuable in God's eyes today as we were when we were born." He urged us to "commit each day into His hands and take delight in the good things He gives."

◆

I have been young, and now am old;
Yet I have not seen the righteous forsaken.

PSALM 37:25

◆

The silver-haired head is a crown of glory,
If it is found in the way of righteousness.

PROVERBS 16:31

The New Testament says nothing of Apostles who retired and took it easy.

Mr. Graham advised seniors who were approaching retirement and worried about feeling useless to invest in life planning. Financial planning was not enough, he said. They also needed to decide how they would spend the remaining years God gave them. With all the advances in medical technology, they could live a third of their lives retired.

Graham recommended an ABC approach:

"Accept the fact that you are retired." He encouraged retirees not to dwell on the past but to look forward to a fresh chapter of life that could bring new adventures.

"Believe that God loves you." The Lord has promised to be with and guide His people throughout their entire lives.

"Commit your life to Jesus Christ, and then ask Him to guide you and use you." Graham pointed out the many options that may open during retirement: volunteer work, church activities, part-time employment, new hobbies, or more family time.

"Don't waste these years," Graham concluded. "Boredom vanishes when we do His will."

◆

Let us not grow weary while doing good, for in
due season we shall reap if we do not lose heart.
Therefore, as we have opportunity, let us do good to all.

GALATIANS 6:9-10

I have discovered that just because we grow weaker physically as we age, it doesn't mean we must grow weaker spiritually.

BILLY GRAHAM

He would never mention names, of course, but Mr. Graham clearly took issue with the idea that anyone—let alone clergymen—should ever let their spiritual lives slide, even if they had retired from ministry. "You don't retire from loving and serving God."

People in his orbit worried about how he might occupy his time after his son Franklin took over the leadership of the Billy Graham Evangelistic Association in 2000. Mr. Graham was approaching his eighty-second birthday and was not well. He had undergone prostate surgery and been diagnosed with Parkinson's—later determined to be hydrocephalus.

Ruth Graham's health had also begun to fail, so Mr. Graham helped look after her as he was able.

He did miss preaching, though he did not miss the attendant travel and media obligations. His inner circle was impressed and gratified that, despite the slower pace, Mr. Graham seemed to relish the extra time at home, which also allowed him to pursue his obsession with keeping up with world events.

In and out of hospitals for various ailments and sometimes confined to a hospital bed even in his own home, Graham followed the news and was eager to discuss geopolitical events with anyone interested.

"That incredible mind was still there," an acquaintance says. "He loved to frame the news in light of Scripture and talk about what it seemed God was up to. He also watched a lot of television, and besides the news, he enjoyed seeing other men preach. It wasn't uncommon for him to phone or write a pastor with compliments on his message."

He looked forward to the rare opportunities to still preach, and his last crusade was in 2005 in New York City, where he spoke to nearly a quarter of a million people. He had to be helped to the pulpit, and his voice was only an echo of what it had once been. But people seemed to love the old lion of the faith, and thousands responded to his invitations to receive Christ as Savior.

◆

I have become as a wonder to many,
But You are my strong refuge.
Let my mouth be filled with Your praise
And with Your glory all the day.
Do not cast me off in the time of old age;
Do not forsake me when my strength fails.

PSALM 71:7-9

Growing old has
been the greatest
surprise of my life.

BILLY GRAHAM

There are no two ways about it: Anyone who knew Billy Graham knew he was a hypochondriac. Even Ruth teased him about it. "Every cold or bout with the flu was certain to be the end of him," she'd say with a smile. "And if he had to go in for something more serious, he'd remind me of his funeral wishes."

But Ruth was alarmed when her husband joked about Parkinson's. He said, "Your handwriting gets illegible and your sermons get longer."

"I didn't find Parkinson's a laughing matter," Ruth said. "My husband became an old man overnight."

For his part, while Mr. Graham became more convinced than ever that his end was near, he often said he didn't fear death. "It's the dying part that worries me."

Yet even after his diagnosis and the struggles that followed, the old evangelist crafted a message for others in the same predicament: First, he said, "accept the fact that you will die." Second, "make arrangements." Third, "make provision for those you are leaving behind." Finally, "make an appointment with God."

But to a friend he quipped, "Don't get old if you can avoid it."

◆

Even to your old age, I am He,
And even to gray hairs I will carry you!
I have made, and I will bear;
Even I will carry, and will deliver you.

ISAIAH 46:4

◆

When I am old and grayheaded,
O God, do not forsake me,
Until I declare Your strength to this generation,
Your power to everyone who is to come.

PSALM 71:18

Every human is under construction from conception to death.

BILLY GRAHAM

Throughout his exhaustive and exhausting ministry, Mr. Graham often insisted that life was just as hard, if not harder, on Ruth. It fell on her to serve as both mother and father. Ruth never complained publicly. In fact, she said she wouldn't have had it any other way. She became the epitome of Billy's lifelong helpmate, supporting him and providing everything he needed to fulfill his calling. She developed her own ministry, producing several volumes of bestselling poetry. And when necessary, she was not afraid to lend her husband advice.

T. W. Wilson, the evangelist's friend since his teens and coworker until his death in 2001 at eighty-two, said, "There would have been no Billy Graham had it not been for Ruth."

Her sense of humor was legendary. Someone once called the house and asked if Mr. Graham was handy. Ruth said, "Not very, but he keeps trying."

Once when Mr. Graham was recounting in an interview how the first woman he proposed to had turned him down, Ruth brought him a box of Kleenex.

He looked puzzled. "Did I ask for these?"

"No," she said, "but you sound like you're about to need 'em."

"Ruth, this happened more than fifty years ago!"

"That's what *I* thought," she said.

When Mrs. Graham's health began to seriously deteriorate as the twenty-first century dawned, she laughed at a sign on the highway and jotted it down. "That's what I want on my tombstone," she told her husband. He thought she was kidding until she also told their son Franklin, by then in charge of the Billy Graham Evangelistic Association.

Her wish was granted, and when she was laid to rest in June 2007, her epitaph read, "End of Construction. Thank you for your patience."

◆

Precious in the sight of the LORD
Is the death of His saints.

PSALM 116:15

The finest Christian
I have ever met?
My wife, Ruth.

BILLY GRAHAM

After his wife's death, it was not uncommon for family, caretakers, or friends to find Mr. Graham just sitting and gazing at a painting of Ruth, sometimes for hours. He didn't seem depressed or morose. He simply missed her terribly and enjoyed reminding himself of her many sterling qualities.

"She was a spiritual giant," he'd say. "Her knowledge of the Bible put mine to shame, and her commitment to prayer was an inspiring challenge to anyone who knew her." One of his favorite memories, he said, was of her sitting on the front porch at sunrise, reading her Bible, her routine for years. "And every night I was home, we held hands and prayed before we went to sleep."

Mr. Graham's obsession with holding Ruth's hand was legendary. Often when he was being driven home from the airport after a trip, he would ask that someone drive Ruth to the local Cracker Barrel restaurant. The moment he saw her, he looked like a teenager in love for the first time. They sat holding hands while waiting for their order.

"I was away too much, but Ruth handled our children with great love and discipline. She believed it was her calling and that my work simply would not have been possible if she had not taken the lion's share of raising the children. She spent hours every week teaching them the Bible and praying with them. She also was full of fun. Life was never dull with Ruth around."

Ruth Graham loved sports and was adventurous. Years ago, after she'd rigged up a small zip line for some of her grandchildren, she tried it first to test it. When it broke, she fell about fifteen feet and fractured several bones, including a vertebra. She also developed peripheral neuropathy and was never the same physically after that.

Mr. Graham recalled that for years Ruth was in and out of hospitals with severe back pain and other ailments. "But she remained a gentle, smiling, kind woman whose goal was to live for Christ and reflect His love. In her last days, she talked repeatedly of Heaven, and although I miss her more than I can say, I rejoice that someday we will be reunited in the presence of the Lord she loved and served so faithfully."

◆

Husbands ought to love their own wives as their
own bodies; he who loves his wife loves himself.
For no one ever hated his own flesh, but nourishes
and cherishes it, just as the Lord does the church.

EPHESIANS 5:28-29

As I got older,
I found myself
becoming more mellow,
more forgiving,
more loving.

BILLY GRAHAM

Recordings of Billy Graham's sermons from the late 1940s and early 1950s reveal stark contrasts to his messages from later years. A biographical researcher, with access to the entire corpus of the Graham audio and visual history, was struck by the evolution. The young evangelist who saw the Los Angeles meetings explode from a scheduled three weeks to eight was a shouting, theatrical, dramatic spellbinder with as much to say about America, patriotism, and anti-communism as about the Gospel.

When the young Graham reached the biblical portion of his sermons, he settled into his celebrated emphasis on one's need for salvation. He left no doubt that spiritual rebirth was his point. But within just a few years, his emphasis became clear from word one. He began with a recitation of society's ills and the ways they impacted the individual, followed by a piercing recognition of one's loneliness, emptiness, sinfulness, and desperate need to be loved and forgiven.

Over the decades, the evangelist's rapid-fire delivery slowed and his tone softened, but the magnetic passion of his voice remained a trademark. Countless admirers told how his aura of authority and conviction captivated them, drew them, and caused them to respond to the Spirit of God when Mr. Graham invited them to come forward.

With less emphasis on judgment and more on love and grace and acceptance, he would plead, "How do you know God won't accept you just as you are? The answer is—You don't! . . . God doesn't wait until we clean up our lives before He lets us come to Him. He accepts us just as we are!

"We can't understand that kind of love. It's not the way we act toward one another. It's supernatural. God's love is an everlasting love—and all He requires is that we turn to Him in repentance and faith and put our trust in Jesus Christ for our salvation. He died in our place."

◆

In Him we have redemption through
His blood, the forgiveness of sins.
EPHESIANS 1:7

I don't need a successor,
only willing hands
to accept the torch for
a new generation.

BILLY GRAHAM

Speculation about who might become the "next Billy Graham" arose by the time the evangelist reached his sixties, and it only increased as the new century dawned and Graham reached his eighties. It wasn't simply about who would succeed him as head of the Billy Graham Evangelistic Association (BGEA). It was about who could captivate massive stadium crowds around the world.

Graham had many devotees among preachers, including some who copied his every strategy. And while many drew huge crowds, none reached his standard of effectiveness. Billy grew tired of the discussion and insisted that all believers were called to share the Gospel. Privately he worried how his own son Franklin might hold up under such comparisons. "We have different gifts," the elder would say. "He has many that I don't have."

In truth, Mr. Graham was determined to stay out of the search for his successor within the organization. He confided to a friend that Ruth believed Franklin should head the ministry. "I knew he could do it," Graham said, "but I didn't want to force it on the board. When they came to the same conclusion as Ruth, I was very pleased."

Franklin, who had been a prodigal as a young man, had found his way back to his faith and become a man of wide interests and abilities. Mr. Graham himself acknowledged his daughter Anne as the "best preacher in the family," but Franklin stepped into the top role at BGEA in 2000 and has expertly led the organization.

"I am both proud of his capacity for leadership and humbled in gratitude for the Lord's blessing on him," Mr. Graham said. "But we need more than just someone to take my place. We need a whole lot of someones to do their part."

◆

I heard the voice of the Lord, saying:

"Whom shall I send,
And who will go for Us?"

Then I said, "Here am I! Send me."

ISAIAH 6:8

Death wasn't part of
God's original plan for
humanity, and the Bible
calls death an enemy—
the last enemy to
be destroyed.

BILLY GRAHAM

Often teased by family and friends for seeming to obsess over his death, Mr. Graham argued, "To never think about death isn't only unrealistic—it's foolish."

The problem was, the evangelist seemed to anticipate it too soon. One of his daughters said it was "as if he knew something we didn't, and so I didn't expect him to live much longer either."

In fact, people in Mr. Graham's orbit began predicting that each succeeding health crisis would likely be the end of him. They said, sometimes publicly, that he was fading, failing, and his eyes were locked on Heaven. A visit to the hospital or to the Mayo Clinic prompted death vigils and plans for the worst.

Yet he lingered for at least a decade longer than most expected—certainly longer than *he* expected. During this time, he wrote books about his last days, as well as about Heaven. He also spoke of looking forward to reuniting with Ruth. His maladies grew worse; he lost his hearing, and his vision faltered. But his mind remained sharp, and he continued to be curious, thoughtful, and engaged. Eventually, his daughter Anne said she had to speak into a microphone and he had to wear earphones to hear her. "But still he asked where I'd been, how things had gone, and whether I had greeted old friends for him. He kept up with my ministry."

One of his themes became the fact that there was no reason for anyone to fear death. "Jesus Christ came into the world to overcome death's power."

◆

He will swallow up death forever,
And the Lord GOD will wipe away tears from all faces;
The rebuke of His people
He will take away from all the earth;
For the LORD has spoken.

ISAIAH 25:8

◆

Then shall be brought to pass the saying that is
written: "Death is swallowed up in victory."

"O Death, where is your sting?
O Hades, where is your victory?"

The sting of death is sin, and the strength of sin
is the law. But thanks be to God, who gives us
the victory through our Lord Jesus Christ.

1 CORINTHIANS 15:54-57

I look forward
to death with great
anticipation, to meeting
God face-to-face.

BILLY GRAHAM

It was not uncommon for Billy Graham to tell interviewers that he did not fear death, though he also said, "All my life I've been taught how to die," he said, "but no one ever taught me how to grow old."

Of course, even those with rock-solid assurance of their eternal destiny would rather avoid the ravaging of the body so many endure at the ends of their lives. Mr. Graham suffered many ailments, but thankfully not to the extent he could have. In the end, he died peacefully in his sleep. It was the kind of exit he had hoped and prayed for. But throughout his final decade, he soldiered on, facing each health crisis as it came, keeping his focus on that "blessed hope": meeting God and seeing Jesus.

Throughout his ministry, Graham taught from the Bible, which says that as sinners we cannot see God's face. He pointed to two Scriptures that describe God as "of purer eyes than to see evil and cannot look at wrong" (Habakkuk 1:13, ESV) and as One who "dwells in unapproachable light, whom no one has ever seen or can see" (1 Timothy 6:16, ESV). Yet Mr. Graham also cited several passages of Scripture that promised the believer would eventually behold God. "That's the great future promise. That's what I want. Matthew 5:8 says, 'Blessed are the pure in heart, for they shall see God.'"

That, Mr. Graham said, "is how I know that in Heaven we will see Jesus Christ face-to-face. Of course, God the Father has no physical form. But apparently we will see and behold God's glory, His radiance, His brilliance. I think we will really be able to understand this only when we experience it. The wonder of it is too far beyond anything we have experienced here on Earth.

"God's glory terrifies the sinner, but it's the deepest longing of the redeemed."

◆

They shall see His face, and His name shall be on their foreheads. There shall be no night there: They need no lamp nor light of the sun, for the Lord God gives them light. And they shall reign forever and ever.

Then [the angel] said to me,
"These words are faithful and true."

REVELATION 22:4-6

I haven't written
my own epitaph, and
I'm not sure I should.
Whatever it is, I hope it
will be simple, and that it
will point people not to me,
but to the One I served.

BILLY GRAHAM

Franklin Graham quoted his father, "I'm prepared to die, in fact I'm looking forward to it—and when you're prepared to die, you're also prepared to live."

Franklin explained on *Today*: "When my mother passed away, we knew what she wanted on her tombstone [see page 86]. I asked my father, so there wouldn't be any argument among us children, 'Daddy, what do you want on your tombstone?' . . . He said, 'Preacher.'

"He spent his life telling people about Heaven, how to get to Heaven. He wrote books on Heaven. Now he's in Heaven," Franklin added. And what would Billy Graham want his son to tell those watching? "If you put your faith and trust in God's Son, Jesus Christ, [then] you can be in Heaven too," Franklin said.

And lest there be any question, Franklin directed that his father's epitaph read:

BILLY GRAHAM

November 7, 1918–February 21, 2018

Preacher of the Gospel
of the Lord Jesus Christ

JOHN 14:6

◆

*Jesus said to him, "I am the way,
the truth, and the life. No one comes
to the Father except through Me."*

JOHN 14:6

PART FIVE

HEAVEN

As long as we are here
on earth, we are strangers
in a foreign land. ... Our
citizenship is in Heaven.

BILLY GRAHAM

With Mr. Graham in Heaven, it's hard to ignore the many comments about his eternal destiny. Many have quipped that the reception line for him in glory, made up merely of those who trace their salvation to his ministry, would take him half of eternity to navigate.

"This world is not my home," begins the song Jim Reeves made famous in the 1960s. "I'm just a-passin' through."* That reflected Graham's outlook; in fact, the older he got, the more the evangelist spoke of paradise.

If you want to imagine Heaven, Mr. Graham said, "think of a place where there will be no sorrow and no parting, no pain, no sickness, no death, no quarrels, no misunderstandings, no sin and no cares."

Graham admitted that his view of the afterlife had matured over the decades. He said, "I once thought and preached that in Heaven we were going to sit around the fireplace and have parties, and the angels would wait on us, and we'd drive down the golden streets in a yellow Cadillac convertible." Now, he said, he believed we might even be assigned tasks in Heaven. "Imagine evangelizing worlds unknown."

---

* Written by Mary Reeves Davis and Albert E. Brumley, copyright © 1965, Sony/ATV Music Publishing LLC.

He admitted that as a young man he had preached "with much more fire and vigor," seeing things as black and white. He attributed it to youthfulness, intensity, conviction, and partly ignorance. Mr. Graham told a magazine reporter in 1994, "I'm definitely more tolerant [now]."

◆

*Our citizenship is in heaven, from which we also
eagerly wait for the Savior, the Lord Jesus Christ,
who will transform our lowly body that
it may be conformed to His glorious body,
according to the working by which He is able
even to subdue all things to Himself.*

PHILIPPIANS 3:20-21

I'm going to Heaven
just like the thief on
the cross who said
in that last moment,
"Lord, remember me."

BILLY GRAHAM

The evangelist said that the Bible doesn't answer all our questions about Heaven because it is "far more wonderful and glorious than our limited minds can fully grasp! Someday we'll see Heaven in all of its glory—but in the meantime (as the Bible says) 'we see only a reflection as in a mirror. . . . Now I know in part; then I shall know fully' (1 Corinthians 13:12, NIV)."

But Mr. Graham believed that what the Bible *does* tell us about Heaven should make us long to be there. For instance, we know that the burdens and disappointments of this life will be no more. Graham acknowledged the challenges of aging and quoted Revelation 21:4: "There shall be no more death, nor sorrow, nor crying. There shall be no more pain, for the former things have passed away."

Like the thief crucified next to Jesus, we've done nothing to earn salvation, but because of His death and resurrection, Heaven will one day be our home. There "we will see Christ in all His glory, and then we'll fully understand the depth of His love and His sacrifice."

◆

[The thief on the cross said], "This Man has done nothing wrong." Then he said to Jesus, "Lord, remember me when You come into Your kingdom."

LUKE 23:41-42

The most thrilling thing about Heaven is that Jesus Christ will be there.

BILLY GRAHAM

The same familiarity with God that had so impressed Ruth Graham the first time she encountered Billy flavored his conversations when he spoke of Heaven. The evangelist enjoyed citing the fact that when the apostle John was given a glimpse of Jesus in Heaven, the beloved disciple was so overwhelmed that he "fell at His feet as dead" (Revelation 1:17).

"Heaven is glorious because it is absolutely perfect." Mr. Graham contrasted that with the sin, decay, and death all around us now. Our world is constantly rocked by wars, natural disasters, and cruelty. He pointed to passages like Micah 4:3, which picture the world at peace: "Nation will not take up sword against nation, nor will they train for war anymore" (NIV).

"Heaven is glorious most of all," said Graham, "because it is the dwelling place of God." He pointed to Revelation 21:3: "Look! God's dwelling place is now among the people, and he will dwell with them" (NIV).

Mr. Graham assured those who wrote him with questions about Heaven that, thanks to Christ, there is a remedy for the sin that separates us from God and our eternal home: "Jesus Christ came to open Heaven's door for us, and He did this by taking upon Himself the judgment that we deserve. Why not put your faith and trust in Him today?"

◆

The grace of God that brings salvation has appeared to all men, teaching us that, denying ungodliness and worldly lusts, we should live soberly, righteously, and godly in the present age, looking for the blessed hope and glorious appearing of our great God and Savior Jesus Christ, who gave Himself for us, that He might redeem us from every lawless deed and purify for Himself His own special people, zealous for good works.

TITUS 2:11-14

PART SIX

LEGACY

The greatest legacy we can pass on to our children and grandchildren is one of character and faith.

Former president of Moody Bible Institute, pastor, and online Bible teacher Dr. Michael Easley says Billy Graham's own children explained why their father's messages resonated with so many people.

They experienced firsthand the way he used both the news and the Bible to communicate God's truth. Graham read Scripture frequently throughout his day. He was also an avid watcher of the evening news. When the program came on, he would quiet the children so he wouldn't miss the reports. When he preached, his understanding of both Scripture and current events was evident. He was a master at helping his listeners see how the two fit together.

Given the constraints of mass communications during the middle of the twentieth century, his ability to tie the two together was "genius," says Easley. "He had this unique skill of taking a very clear message from a passage of Scripture, tying it to today's issues . . . and wrapping the Gospel in a package that was simple for the masses."

Easley adds that as a preacher himself, he listened to Graham and thought, "On one level, it's pretty simple. On the other, it's brilliant the way he sewed it together. He was an extraordinarily gifted communicator, and simple but clear every time."

That all five of Billy and Ruth's children are engaged in ministry today is a testament to Mr. Graham's message and influence on them as well.

♦

I have no greater joy than to hear that
my children walk in truth.

3 JOHN 1:4

Some day you will read in the papers that [I am] dead. Don't you believe a word of it! At that moment I shall be more alive than I am now; I shall have gone up higher, that is all, out of this old clay tenement into a house that is immortal—a body that death cannot touch, that sin cannot taint; a body fashioned like unto His glorious body.

BILLY GRAHAM, QUOTING D. L. MOODY (1837–1899)

"Daddy's home" is how Anne Graham Lotz, the second of his five children, expressed herself shortly after Billy Graham's death. She said he was finally where he had always wanted to be.

Though he'd virtually been on his deathbed for years, the news of his passing came as a surprise to BGEA staff. David Bruce, his administrator of personal affairs for about twenty years, reported that Mr. Graham died in his sleep. He was declared dead at 7:46 a.m., Eastern time, on February 21, 2018, at age ninety-nine.

His personal doctor said, "He just wore out."

Except for occasional short stays in the hospital, Mr. Graham had been under round-the-clock care at home for more than a decade since Ruth had died.

◆

He who hears My word and believes in Him
who sent Me has everlasting life, and shall not come
into judgment, but has passed from death into life.

JOHN 5:24

Believers,
look up—take courage.
The angels are nearer
than you think.

BILLY GRAHAM

Wayne Atcheson, director and regional manager for the Billy Graham Library since 2006, has led more than 10,000 people on tours of the place. He says, "I often prayed Mr. Graham would live to be one hundred, but God was ready for him."

Atcheson was with about 250 people in staff devotions the morning of February 22 when Graham's death was announced. "I must admit," he says, "after telling people about his life and ministry for twelve years, I was deeply saddened. I felt as if I was trying to catch my breath all day."

Atcheson, who estimates he shares about 200 facts and anecdotes during each tour, adds, "There's nothing greater than telling about the life of a man who preached the Gospel more than any man since the days of Christ. You can't beat that."

The library's director says that, as he gives tours, he often feels as if he is giving a sermon or presenting the Gospel as Graham might have done. Atcheson sees his job as a tremendous privilege: "I call it the dessert of my career."

◆

For a day in Your courts is
better than a thousand.
I would rather be a doorkeeper
in the house of my God
Than dwell in the tents of wickedness.
For the LORD God is a sun and shield;
The LORD will give grace and glory;
No good thing will He withhold
From those who walk uprightly.

PSALM 84:10-11

The love of God
is absolute. . . . He loves
everybody regardless of
what label they have.

BILLY GRAHAM

By the time of his passing, Mr. Graham's legacy had been fully established. After so many decades of public ministry, only the spiritually blind and deaf could have missed his message: salvation by grace through faith alone.

But he had also staked out his conviction that the Bible was the authoritative Word of God, and he had preached with that assumption since 1949. Though criticized in some quarters for having no theological degrees, Graham considered himself a lifelong student of the Bible and the Gospel as good news to the "lost and those confused about purpose and meaning in life."

The more he traveled, the more he urged Christians of all denominations to "love one another." He liked to point out that, "Jesus did not only say that whoever was not for Him was against Him (Matthew 12:30), but also that whoever was not against Him was *for* Him (Luke 9:50)." That, to Mr. Graham, made clear that believers ought to be more inclusive and less judgmental. "It isn't that doctrinal differences and distinctives don't matter. They do. But many well-meaning believers may be off base on some theological issue and still be considered *for* Christ."

The love of God became the heart of Mr. Graham's

message, and he preached that Jesus' sacrifice on the cross dealt with both the sins of the world and individuals' sins.

Andrew Finstuen, dean of the Honors College and associate professor of history at Boise State University, says that "Graham never wavered in his primary mission to bring individuals to Christ. But he worried less about—as he preached in 1949—'the sins of the Sunset Strip,' and more about social problems, including racism, AIDS, and poverty.

"The legacies of Graham's ministry are many, but perhaps none is greater than its demonstration that it is not the flames of hell but the triumphant love of God that defines and emboldens a Christian life."

♦

If we live, we live to the Lord;
and if we die, we die to the Lord.
Therefore, whether we live or die, we are the Lord's.

ROMANS 14:8

The apostle Paul told the Corinthians that he felt called to be all things to all people. Yet I realized I had closed myself to the people of the Soviet Union.

BILLY GRAHAM

Another major element of Billy Graham's legacy was his prescience in his attitude toward the communist world. In the 1940s and 1950s he railed against communism and its godless atheism. Yet in 1982 he accepted an invitation to a peace conference in Moscow, much to the displeasure of many in Washington. The Cold War was in full swing, and even some of Mr. Graham's friends, such as Vice President George H. W. Bush, predicted he would be exploited and used as a propaganda boost to Soviet leadership. His visit, some felt, would bolster the Soviets' claim that they respected religious freedom.

Graham is on record, however, that he had been briefed by the Pentagon about what could happen, yet he believed only good could come from his going. After the fall of communism, then-President George H. W. Bush told the National Religious Broadcasters in 1990, "Eight years ago, one of the Lord's great ambassadors, Rev. Billy Graham, went to Eastern Europe and the Soviet Union and, upon returning, spoke of a movement there toward more religious freedom. And perhaps he saw it before many of us because it takes a man of God to sense the early movement of the hand of God."

◆

*To the weak I became as weak, that I might win
the weak. I have become all things to all men,
that I might by all means save some.*

1 CORINTHIANS 9:22

[Jesus] used all the technology of His day to reach people, and He certainly would have used technology today.

BILLY GRAHAM

For more than half of Billy Graham's public ministry, Larry Ross was his director of media and public relations as well as his spokesperson.

Ross says that after virtually every crusade during Mr. Graham's final ten years of preaching, "local media would report that it was Graham's last." Ross deduces that this may have been because the progress of technology had begun to accelerate at such a blistering pace that each subsequent crusade reached more people on a scale capable of spanning the entire globe.

Graham had always engaged with the press—which Ross believed expanded his influence far beyond the audiences at his crusades. In addition, his ministry adopted technological advances early, which made Graham "a media pioneer as much as an evangelist."

Mr. Graham was once asked if Jesus were still on Earth, would He use the technologies available now. He said Jesus taught "by walking and telling stories . . . and illustrating the message He wanted to get across." Ross believes Graham was saying Jesus also understood the power of story and had found a way to ensure His message would "go viral."

A major part of Mr. Graham's legacy was his recognition of the potential of the Internet. He believed it would have a huge impact on evangelism, and of course he was right.

Ross points out that Billy Graham used every medium at his disposal from the beginning of his ministry. Whether newsprint, books, radio, television, or film, "Graham always sought platforms, not publicity, for his message."

◆

The disciples came and said to Him,
"Why do You speak to them in parables?"

He answered and said to them, "Because it has been
given to you to know the mysteries of the kingdom
of heaven, but to them it has not been given."

MATTHEW 13:10-11

I don't travel with,
meet with, or dine alone
with an unrelated female.

BILLY GRAHAM

Longtime BGEA crusade director Rick Marshall says Mr. Graham "was a risk-taker, who was willing to go where no one else had gone, in being among the first to leverage new mediums" for his message. Steve Case, cofounder of America Online (AOL), notes, "When radio became important, he started buying radio stations. When motion pictures were important, he started creating movies. . . . When television became important, he leveraged television. And of course, the Internet as well."

Graham spokesman, Larry Ross, says he "put his biblical message into a cultural context, using language and illustrations he knew would best appeal to his audience." Though Graham didn't consider himself anyone special, he understood the significance of name recognition.

That led to another significant aspect of Graham's legacy, according to Ross. Graham's ministry, which lasted more than six decades, was scandal-free. When other notable preachers fell into disrepute, Graham carefully guarded his team from any whiff of impropriety.

When several television preachers were hit with scandal during the late 1980s, Graham received more than 350 requests for interviews about televangelism. He turned them all down, instead referring inquirers to his book *A Biblical Standard for Evangelists.*

That book originated in 1948, when Billy was coming up to his thirtieth birthday. He and his small ministry team, which included assistant evangelist Grady Wilson, singer George Beverly Shea, and song leader Cliff Barrows, met for Bible study and prayer at a tiny motel in Modesto, California. Graham challenged them to pray about the codes of behavior they needed to adopt in order to keep the ministry clean.

The results proved profound and prophetic. They outlined what would become known as the Modesto Manifesto. This same list of core ministry values was adopted by the Billy Graham Evangelistic Association when it was founded a few years later.

The Modesto Manifesto included four components:

Honesty: Size of crowds and number of inquirers were not to be embellished or exaggerated.

Integrity: A board of directors would review expenditures. Every crusade would open its books and publish where and how all monies were spent.

Purity: To avoid temptation, each team member
 agreed never to be alone with another woman,
 to be accountable to one another and their wives,
 and to help the wives feel part of the crusades.
Humility: The team would never disparage other
 Christian ministers, regardless of their affiliation
 or theological views.

◆

Abstain from all appearance of evil.
1 THESSALONIANS 5:22, KJV

God has given us moral
and spiritual rules—
not to restrict us, but
to protect us. He knows
the dangers we face, and
He loves us too much to
let us live any way we want.

BILLY GRAHAM

From the correspondence that poured into his ministry over the years, Mr. Graham could see that many people had been caught in a trap, believing they were free to do anything they wanted without suffering any consequences. "God says otherwise," Mr. Graham would tell them, "and every day I get letters from people who've discovered this through bitter experience."

His friends and acquaintances often told of how Graham scrupulously protected himself from the very dangers the Modesto Manifesto aimed to counter. Normal business lunches with him were planned well in advance, and guests were ushered to a prearranged spot. If not in a private room, the table was discreetly located, usually close to a back or side entrance so Mr. Graham's arrival would create no stir.

To avoid even an appearance of impropriety, one or two members of Graham's staff were always present, no more than a few feet away. The team took every precaution to preclude anyone trying to discredit Mr. Graham or the ministry by rushing a woman up to him and snapping a photo.

An interviewer riding to an impromptu lunch with him saw Graham's driver panic when the evangelist quickly exited the car to see how long a restaurant's wait time was. Customers in a line that extended outside immediately recognized him as he disappeared inside. The interviewer says the driver leapt from the haphazardly stopped car and gave chase.

He found Mr. Graham chatting with the maître d'. The driver told the interviewer, "He's my responsibility today, and I almost let him get away!"

Mr. Graham insisted the restaurant make no fuss and he be given no special treatment, but arrangements were quickly made to accommodate his party.

"He was sincere about this," the driver said, "not realizing that everyone waiting in line would have eagerly given up their place for us. That's why our custom is to plan so far ahead."

◆

Be careful to obey all these regulations
. . . so that it may always go well with you
and your children after you, because you
will be doing what is good and right.

DEUTERONOMY 12:28, NIV

The cross shows us the
seriousness of our sin—
but it also shows us the
immeasurable love of God.

BILLY GRAHAM

With the message of Christ's death and resurrection motivating him to the end of his ministry, Mr. Graham also left a legacy as an innovator. Shortly after his death, *Christianity Today*—itself the brainchild of Billy Graham—published a list of the many organizations he had founded or to which he provided key support.

Besides his own evangelistic association and *Christianity Today*, Graham helped launch Youth for Christ (he was its first full-time evangelist). He became Wheaton College's most celebrated alum, served for a time as the youngest US college president at Northwestern Bible College in Minnesota, and helped establish Gordon-Conwell Theological Seminary in Massachusetts. He also supported the development of Greater Europe Mission, TransWorld Radio, World Vision, World Relief, the National Association of Evangelicals, and the Evangelical Council for Financial Accountability.

Mr. Graham hosted global conferences that helped unify evangelicals: the 1966 World Congress on Evangelism (Berlin), the 1974 International Congress on World Evangelization (Lausanne, Switzerland), and three conferences for itinerant evangelists in Amsterdam

(1983, 1986, and 2000), which attracted nearly 24,000 people from 200 countries. For the first conference in Amsterdam, Graham's ministry brought almost 4,000 itinerant preachers from 133 countries to Amsterdam for nine days, picking up almost all the expenses. Twice as many evangelists came three years later; once again the Billy Graham Evangelistic Ministry funded the conference.

Graham's innovations continued late into his career. In the 1990s he reengineered his crusades, morphing his customary youth night into a "Concert for the Next Generation." These events drew record crowds of young people who came not only to hear Graham preach but to listen to Christian rock, rap, and hip-hop artists.

Billy Graham's legacy continues through those ministers he trained from around the globe. His longtime media representative, Larry Ross, says his influence "has been so broad, and his impact so far-reaching, we won't know this side of heaven the extent of his legacy."

Theologian J. I. Packer credits Mr. Graham with what he calls the evangelical "convergence." He notes that "evangelicals came together behind [him] and the things he stood for."

LEGACY

◆

*The things that you have heard from me among
many witnesses, commit these to faithful men
who will be able to teach others also.*

2 TIMOTHY 2:2

God has given us two
hands, one to receive with
and the other to give with.

BILLY GRAHAM

Rick Marshall, the former BGEA crusade director, admired Billy Graham's desire to continue learning. Not only did he study the culture, he "was constantly looking for philosophies and politics; and words and phrases; stories and people; and illustrations that he could use to open a window into the human heart."

In 1963, the Billy Graham Evangelistic Association contacted Kenneth Taylor to see if they could use his paraphrase of Paul's epistles, *The Living Letters*, as their first-ever TV giveaway. Taylor, who had founded Tyndale House Publishers the previous year after he was unable to find a publisher for the book, readily agreed. Eventually, the BGEA sent out about 600,000 copies.

In the coming years, Taylor paraphrased the rest of the Bible and in 1971 released *The Living Bible*. It has sold well over 40 million copies.

Mark Taylor, Kenneth's son and the current chairman and CEO of Tyndale House, says, "Mr. Graham was criticized for encouraging people to read a paraphrase of the New Testament, but he recognized the value of a translation that reads 'like today's newspaper.'" Indeed, although *The Living Bible* was the result of untold hours of toil by Kenneth Taylor, Mr. Graham first put it on the map.

◆

Lay up for yourselves treasures in heaven,
where neither moth nor rust destroys
and where thieves do not break in
and steal. For where your treasure is,
there your heart will be also.

MATTHEW 6:20-21

The word of the
Lord has come unto me,
and He tells me to go
and proclaim His Gospel
as long as I have breath.

BILLY GRAHAM

According to former Moody Bible Institute president Dr. Michael J. Easley, Mr. Graham was blessed in a special way.

While Easley says many people point to Graham's communication skills and simply "being in the right place at the right time" as the keys to his success, "I have to believe it was the work of God in the man's life and His hand on him as a servant in a unique way."

Easley said one thing in particular struck him as he watched all the news footage of Graham shown after his death. "Watching the clips, how often do you see Jesus mentioned? Not [just] God. Jesus. He was very clear in his Christology, in understanding the Gospel, and in how to present it simply to the masses."

Asked what he thought differentiated his ministry message from that of other preachers, Mr. Graham told an interviewer, "I don't think that way. I appreciate anyone who shares the Gospel. But I did find from the time I began preaching as a college student in Florida that if I put the emphasis on Jesus, God's Spirit would do the rest."

◆

*How beautiful upon the mountains
Are the feet of him who brings good news,
Who proclaims peace,
Who brings glad tidings of good things,
Who proclaims salvation.*

ISAIAH 52:7

The Bible passes
every test that can
be applied to it.

BILLY GRAHAM

Another shining example of Billy Graham's legacy was his high view of Scripture.

As early as the mid-1950s, Carl F. H. Henry, the first editor of *Christianity Today* magazine, wrote that the evangelist had none of the "half-hearted confidence in the reliability and authority of Scripture" that characterized the nonevangelical theologian Karl Barth. "Nobody has profounder right than Mr. Graham to a hearing on the subject of the authority of the Bible in evangelistic preaching. He has earned that right theoretically, by his devout study of the Word, and pragmatically, by his passionate proclamation of it to an age of theological unbelief."

Edward J. Carnell, a noted neoevangelical of that time, said of Graham, "After [he] has reviewed the plan of salvation, he has very little to add. Billy Graham has not been to seminary. He has no criteria by which to measure the shades of better and worse in the complex systems which vie for the modern mind. . . . [Yet] Billy Graham preaches Christ in such clear and forceful language that even a bartender can find his way to the mercy seat. This is why the multitudes discover a power in Billy Graham. . . . Graham may know little about the inner technicalities of theology, but he does rest in the full and undoubted persuasion that Christ was delivered for our offenses and was raised for our justification."

Graham said Jesus Himself was his example for seeing the Scriptures as the authoritative Word of God (Matthew 4:4-10) and declared that their authority could not be broken. "The more you study the Bible, the more you become aware that it is God's Word because of the transformation it makes in the lives of those who live by its teaching.

"It is God's own Word, His saving truth which He has spoken to mankind. It is inspired from beginning to end, and it is the only infallible guide of faith and practice."

◆

The Scripture cannot be broken.

JOHN 10:35

Courage is contagious.
When a brave man takes
a stand, the spines of
others are often stiffened.

BILLY GRAHAM

Billy Graham took a bold step for civil rights long before integration was accepted. He was way ahead of most white preachers, especially those from the South. In the early 1950s, Jim Crow laws were still in effect in many Southern states. They made no sense to Mr. Graham, and he insisted that all his meetings, no matter where they were held, be integrated. He himself took down the barrier separating the races at his crusade in Jackson, Mississippi, in 1952. Detractors predicted disaster, but blacks and whites sat together, and not one negative incident was reported.

Not long after, the evangelist publicly lauded the efforts of Martin Luther King Jr. and had him pray at some crusades. Once he even bailed King out of jail.

"There is no scriptural basis for segregation," Mr. Graham said. He pointed out that God created every human being—regardless of their race—in His image. And Christ died for people "of every tribe and tongue and people and nation" (Revelation 5:9).

Mr. Graham believed racism was the greatest social problem the world faced, leading to injustice, poverty, and wars throughout the world. Why was it such a long-standing scourge? "Racism has its roots in human pride and sin," he said, "and these will never be completely erased until Christ comes again." Even so, "that shouldn't keep us from reaching out and trying to eliminate the barriers that divide us," he said.

"We're a diverse society, and the media shows both the discord but also that we can get along, and that's marvelous."

♦

Let nothing be done through selfish ambition or conceit, but in lowliness of mind let each esteem others better than himself. Let each of you look out not only for his own interests, but also for the interests of others.

PHILIPPIANS 2:3-4

I hope I will be remembered as someone who was faithful—faithful to God, faithful to the Gospel of Jesus Christ and faithful to the calling God gave me.

BILLY GRAHAM

More than two decades before he died, Billy Graham told an interviewer about his final syndicated newspaper column, already written and to be released upon his passing. He assumed his death would happen within a few years, not realizing that he still had a quarter century to live.

He said he was determined to leave one last invitation "for men and women and boys and girls to receive Christ as their Savior before it's too late."

In that column Mr. Graham wrote, "I'm sure I've failed in many ways, but I take comfort also in Christ's promise of forgiveness, and I take comfort also in God's ability to take even our most imperfect efforts and use them for His glory.

"By the time you read this, I will be in Heaven," Mr. Graham wrote. But he added that he would be there not because he'd lived a good life or had been a famous preacher. Instead, he would be in Heaven because decades before he had trusted in Christ, whose death and resurrection made forgiveness and eternal life in Heaven possible.

He ended his reflection with this challenge to each reader: "Do you know you will go to Heaven when you die? You can, by committing your life to Christ today."

◆

But as it is written:

"Eye has not seen, nor ear heard,
Nor have entered into the heart of man
The things which God has prepared for those who love Him."

1 CORINTHIANS 2:9

◆

Not by works of righteousness which we have done,
but according to His mercy He saved us.

TITUS 3:5

I've read the last page
of the Bible. It's all going
to turn out all right.

BILLY GRAHAM

Mr. Graham loved to speak of the future, and not just of death and Heaven. He was fascinated with biblical prophecy related to the return of Christ. "With so much chaos in the world," he said, "many wonder if we're living in the end times." He encouraged those who were fearful of these coming events to remember John 16:33, where Jesus says, "In the world you will have tribulation. But take heart; I have overcome the world" (ESV).

The evangelist believed the end would be "sudden and unexpected—and most people will be unprepared. Then it will be too late to turn to God." He pointed to the cataclysmic events foretold in 2 Peter 3:10, NIV: "The heavens will disappear with a roar; the elements will be destroyed by fire, and the earth and everything done in it will be laid bare."

Despite that dire warning, many have remarked on how Mr. Graham's eyes twinkled when he went on to tell how the expectation of Christ's coming changed everything. He said, "The good news is, we need not fear that day if we know Christ." And of course, he always returned to his core message and question: "Is your faith and hope in Him, and are you seeking to live for Him every day?" He turned again to Peter's second letter: "Since everything will be destroyed in this way, what kind of people ought you to be? You ought to live holy and godly lives as you look forward to the day of God" (3:11-12, NIV).

♦

Behold, I am coming quickly, and My reward is
with Me, to give to every one according to his work.
I am the Alpha and the Omega, the Beginning
and the End, the First and the Last.

REVELATION 22:12-13

No matter what your problem is, if you and I could sit down and talk, I would want to tell you one great truth: God loves you, and He can make a difference in your life if you will let Him.

BILLY GRAHAM

Perhaps Billy Graham's most lasting legacy will be that he always made his message personal. Sitting in a stadium with 100,000 others, each listener felt as if he were speaking directly to them. His voice was a clarion call piercing the air and resounding through great public address systems. His persuasive, passionate preaching seemed to cut through the troubles of the day and the voices that always justified putting off the things of God until another time.

"The Bible says we're sinners, you and I! We can't save ourselves! But Jesus took your sins upon His own body on the cross, suffered, and died for you."

Praying unceasingly as he preached, as he pleaded, as he invited, and as he watched thousands upon thousands stream forward to receive Christ, Billy Graham lived to share the Gospel.

His simple epitaph embodies the vast breadth of his legacy.

Preacher

♦

I declare to you the gospel which I preached to you,
which also you received and in which you stand,
by which also you are saved, if you hold fast that word
which I preached to you—unless you believed in vain.

For I delivered to you first of all that which I also
received: that Christ died for our sins according to
the Scriptures, and that He was buried, and that He
rose again the third day according to the Scriptures.

1 CORINTHIANS 15:1-4

Acknowledgments

BOOKS ARE NEVER SOLOS. I owe deep debts of gratitude to:

My wife and ever my heart, Dianna,

My agent, the indefatigable Alex Field,

My indispensable assistants, Lynn and Debbie Kaupp, who free me to stay in my lane,

David Loy, Chase Neely, and the Leverage Creative Group,

and Ron Beers and Kim Miller at Tyndale Momentum.

Sources

A. Larry Ross Communications. "Billy Graham." https://static1.square
  space.com/static/546d1bfbe4b0f37a260be87a/t/5a666e24ec212d8
  4589adf56/1516662309512/Billy+Graham+Fact+Sheet.pdf.

Bailey, Laura. "Telling the Story of Billy Graham: 1,000 Times and
  Counting." June 6, 2017. https://billygraham.org/story/telling-the
  -story-of-billy-graham-1000-times-and-counting/. © 2017 Billy
  Graham Evangelistic Association. Used with permission. All rights
  reserved.

Bailey, Sarah Pulliam. "Q & A: Billy Graham on Aging, Regrets, and
  Evangelicals." *Christianity Today*. January 21, 2011. https://www
  .christianitytoday.com/ct/2011/januaryweb-only/qabillygraham
  .html.

Billy Graham Evangelistic Association. "5 Answers from Billy Graham
  on the End Times." August 15, 2017. https://billygraham.org/story
  /5-answers-from-billy-graham-on-the-end-times/. © The Billy
  Graham Literary Trust. Used with permission. All rights reserved.

Billy Graham Evangelistic Association Staff. "Answers." June 1,
  2004. https://billygraham.org/answer/can-we-still-believe-in-the
  -authority-of-the-bible-for-our-modern-world/. © 2004 Billy
  Graham Evangelistic Association. Used with permission. All
  rights reserved.

———. "Answers." February 24, 2014. https://billygraham.org/answer
  /be-on-guard-against-a-self-centered-pride/. © 2014 Billy Graham
  Evangelistic Association. Used with permission. All rights reserved.

Billy Graham Evangelistic Association. *The Cross* video. © 2013 Billy Graham Evangelistic Association. Used with permission. All rights reserved.

Boffey, Matthew. "In Loving Honor: 12 Quotes on Evangelism from Billy Graham." *Logos Talk*, February 21, 2018. https://blog.logos .com/2018/02/loving-honor-12-quotes-evangelism-billy-graham/.

Boyle, John. "Details on Billy Graham's Passing, Funeral Service Released." *USA Today*, February 21, 2018. https://www.usatoday .com/story/news/nation-now/2018/02/21/details-billy-grahams -passing-funeral-service-released/361780002/.

Busby, Russ. *Billy Graham: God's Ambassador*. Alexandria, VA: Time Life Books, 1999.

Carnell, Edward J. "Can Billy Graham Slay the Giant?" *Christianity Today*, May 13, 1957, 4. Quoted in Betty DeBerg. "The Ministry of Christian Art: Evangelicals and the Art of Warner Sallman, 1942–1960." In *Icons of American Protestantism: The Art of Warner Sallman*, edited by David Morgan. New Haven, CT: Yale University Press, 1996.

Christian MARKET Weekly. "Billy Graham 'Changes Addresses.'" CBA. http://cbaonline.org/billy-graham-changes-addresses/.

Davis, Mary Reeves, and Albert E. Brumley. "This World Is Not My Home." Sony/ATV, 1965.

Easley, Michael. "God Chose to Use Him in a Remarkable Way," interviewed by Greg Corombos. Radio America Online News Bureau, February 21, 2018. http://dateline.radioamerica.org /?p=18289.

Fields-Meyer, Thomas. "Rev. Billy Graham: 'I'll Be Happy to Get Out of This Body.'" *People*, June 20, 2005. http://people.com/archive/ rev-billy-graham-ill-be-happy-to-get-out-of-this-body-vol-63- no-24/.

Finstuen, Andrew S. "Sinners in the Hands of a Loving God." *Christianity Today*, April 2018. https://www.christianitytoday.com/ct/2018/billy -graham/sinners-in-hands-of-loving-god-billy-graham-preaching .html.

Funk, Tim and Maria David. "Quotes from Evangelist Billy Graham on Life, Faith, Sin—and His One Regret." *Charlotte Observer*, February 21, 2018. http://www.charlotteobserver.com/news/special -reports/billy-graham-life/article201382089.html.

Gilbreath, Edward. "History in the Making: Billy Graham Had a Dream." Christian History Institute. https://christianhistoryinstitute.org/magazine/article/history-in-the-making-billy-graham-had-a-dream.

Grady, J. Lee. "How Billy Graham Avoided Scandal His Entire Life," Charisma News, March 1, 2018. https://www.charismanews.com/opinion/69841-how-billy-graham-avoided-scandal-his-entire-life.

Graham, Billy. "The ABCs of Your Life after Retirement." Posted on Tribune Media's website, November 25, 2017. https://tribunecontentagency.com/article/the-abcs-of-your-life-after-retirement/. © The Billy Graham Literary Trust. Used with permission. All rights reserved.

———. "Answers." July 27, 2005. Billy Graham Evangelistic Association. https://billygraham.org/answer/do-you-think-our-nation-will-ever-completely-overcome-its-racism/. © The Billy Graham Literary Trust. Used with permission. All rights reserved.

———. "Answers." September 12, 2014. Billy Graham Evangelistic Association. https://billygraham.org/answer/with-faith-in-christ-we-need-not-fear-the-end-of-the-world/. © The Billy Graham Literary Trust. Used with permission. All rights reserved.

———. "Answers." June 5, 2017. Billy Graham Evangelistic Association. https://billygraham.org/answer/what-is-heaven-like/. © The Billy Graham Literary Trust. Used with permission. All rights reserved.

———. "Answers." August 21, 2017. Billy Graham Evangelistic Association. https://billygraham.org/answer/were-retired-and-bored-did-people-retire-in-biblical-days/. © The Billy Graham Literary Trust. Used with permission. All rights reserved.

———. "Answers." September 9, 2017. Billy Graham Evangelistic Association. https://billygraham.org/answer/good-god-forgive/. © The Billy Graham Literary Trust. Used with permission. All rights reserved.

———. "Answers." December 16, 2017. Billy Graham Evangelistic Association. https://billygraham.org/answer/my-husband-turned-50-and-it-hit-him-hard-how-can-i-help-him/. © The Billy Graham Literary Trust. Used with permission. All rights reserved.

———. "Answers." January 6, 2018. Billy Graham Evangelistic Association. https://billygraham.org/answer/what-is-heaven-like-2/. © The Billy Graham Literary Trust. Used with permission. All rights reserved.

———. "Answers." February 14, 2018. Billy Graham Evangelistic Association. https://billygraham.org/answer/why-am-i-so -preoccupied-with-death/. © The Billy Graham Literary Trust. Used with permission. All rights reserved.

———. "Answers." February 21, 2018. Billy Graham Evangelistic Association. https://billygraham.org/answer/billy-grahams-final -answer-wanted-remembered/. © The Billy Graham Literary Trust. Used with permission. All rights reserved.

———. "Billy Graham Quotes." BrainyQuote. https://www.brainy quote.com/quotes/billy_graham_113622.

———. "Billy Graham Quotes." BrainyQuote. https://www.brainy quote.com/quotes/billy_graham_446552.

———. "Death the Enemy." *Decision*, October 5, 2009. https://billy graham.org/decision-magazine/october-2009/death-the-enemy/. From *Hour of Decision* sermon, 1974 Billy Graham Crusade in Virginia. © 1974 Billy Graham Evangelistic Association. Used with permission. All rights reserved.

———. "Faith Produces Works," May 17 devotional, https://billy graham.org/devotion/faith-produces-works/. From *Day by Day with Billy Graham*. Charlotte, North Carolina: Billy Graham Evangelistic Association, 2011. © Billy Graham Evangelistic Association. Used with permission. All rights reserved.

———. *Hear My Heart: What I Would Say to You*. New York: Howard, 2018.

———. *Hope for the Troubled Heart*. Dallas: Word, 1991.

———. *How to Be Born Again*. Waco, Texas: Word, 1977.

———. *The Journey: How to Live by Faith in an Uncertain World*. Nashville: Thomas Nelson, 2006.

———. *Just As I Am*. New York: HarperCollins, 1997.

———. *The Last Crusade*. New York: Berkley, 2005.

———. *Nearing Home: Life, Faith, and Finishing Well*. Nashville: Thomas Nelson, 2013.

Graham, Franklin, and Donna Lee Toney. *Billy Graham in Quotes*. Nashville: Thomas Nelson, 2011.

Hansen, Collin, compiler. "What I Would Have Done Differently." *Christianity Today*, April 2018. https://www.christianitytoday.com /ct/2018/billy-graham/what-i-would-have-done-differently.html.

Harris, Gerald. "Billy Graham's Funeral Plans—An Up Close and Personal
    Look." *The Christian Index*. March 1, 2018. https://christianindex
    .org/billy-grahams-funeral-plans-close-personal-look/.

Henry, Carl F. H. "Evangelism and the Sacred Book," *Christianity Today*.
    October 15, 1956, 23. Quoted in Betty DeBerg. "The Ministry
    of Christian Art: Evangelicals and the Art of Warner Sallman,
    1942–1960." In *Icons of American Protestantism: The Art of Warner
    Sallman*, edited by David Morgan. New Haven, CT: Yale University
    Press, 1996.

Hughes, Becky. "Remembering Billy Graham: His Most Powerful Quotes
    on Life and Spirituality." *Parade*, February 21, 2018. https://parade
    .com/648000/beckyhughes/remembering-billy-graham-his-most
    -powerful-quotes-on-life-and-spirituality/.

Jenkins, Jerry. Personal conversations with Billy Graham from 1974
    through 2008.

Jenkins, Jerry. "Precious Memories: Billy Graham (1918-2018)." https://
    jerryjenkins.com/precious-memories-billy-graham-1918-2018/.

"Jerry Jenkins Shares Lessons Learned from Billy Graham." Colorado
    Christian University. October 12, 2009. https://www.ccu.edu/news
    /2009/jenkins-tributes-billy-graham/.

Kim, Eun Kyung. "Billy Graham's Son Recalls Dad's Final Days: 'We're
    Thrilled His Suffering Is Over.'" *Today*. February 22, 2018.

Kinosian, Janet. "Pilgrim's Progress: Billy Graham on Death, Dying and
    Faith." *HuffPost* (blog), April 25, 2010. https://www.huffingtonpost
    .com/janet-kinosian/pilgrims-progress-billy-g_b_472137.html.

Kumar, Anugrah. "Franklin Graham Reveals What's Written on Billy
    Graham's Grave." *Christian Post*. March 5, 2018. https://www
    .christianpost.com/news/franklin-graham-reveals-whats-written
    -on-billy-grahams-grave-220277/.

McDaniel, Debbie. "40 Courageous Quotes from Evangelist Billy
    Graham." Crosswalk. https://www.crosswalk.com/faith/spiritual
    -life/inspiring-quotes/40-courageous-quotes-from-evangelist-billy
    -graham.html.

Meacham, Jon. "Billy Graham in Twilight: The Christian Evangelist
    Reflects on Politics, Scripture and Mortality in a 2006 Newsweek
    Profile." *Newsweek*, February 21, 2018. http://www.newsweek.com
    /billy-graham-twilight-evangelist-newsweek-profile-815028.

Petre, Jonathan, and Fleur Brennan. "Billy Graham Passes Torch to Followers in 'Great Peace.'" *Telegraph*, July 30, 2000. https://www.telegraph.co.uk/news/worldnews/europe/netherlands/1350965/Billy-Graham-passes-torch-to-followers-in-great-peace.html.

Pokki, Timo. *America's Preacher and His Message*. Lanham, MD: University Press of America, 1999.

Ross, A. Larry. "Billy Graham Leaves a Legacy of Influence." Assist News Service. March 3, 2018. http://assistnews.net/index.php/component/k2/item/3743-billy-graham-leaves-a-legacy-of-influence.

Ross, A. Larry. "Why Billy Graham Was a Media Pioneer as Much as He Was an Evangelist." Fox News, March 1, 2018. http://www.foxnews.com/opinion/2018/03/01/why-billy-graham-was-media-pioneer-as-much-as-was-evangelist.html.

Shelley, Marshall. "Evangelist Billy Graham Has Died." *Christianity Today*, April 2018. https://www.christianitytoday.com/ct/2018/billy-graham/died-billy-graham-obituary.html.

Silverman, Leah. "15 of Billy Graham's Most Powerful Quotes." *Town & Country*, February 21, 2018. https://www.townandcountrymag.com/leisure/arts-and-culture/a18564816/billy-graham-quotes/.

"Simple Message on Billy Graham's Gravestone Shared by Son Franklin." *Christian Today*. March 5, 2018. https://www.christiantoday.com/article/simple-message-on-billy-grahams-gravestone-shared-by-son-franklin/126865.htm.

TobyMac, "City on Our Knees" (video), lyrics by Cary Ryan Barlowe, James L. Moore, and Toby McKeehan. *My Hope: Songs Inspired by the Message and Mission of Billy Graham*. Sparrow, Capitol CMG Label Group, and the Billy Graham Evangelistic Association, 2013.

Wacker, Grant. "How an Aging Billy Graham Approached His Own Death." *Washington Post*, February 21, 2018. https://www.washingtonpost.com/news/acts-of-faith/wp/2018/02/21/how-an-aging-billy-graham-approached-his-own-death/?noredirect=on&utm_term=.e3f50b07bd7e.

Warren, Rick. "Rick Warren: What I Learned from Billy." *Christianity Today*, April 2018. https://www.christianitytoday.com/ct/2018/billy-graham/rick-warren-what-i-learned-from-billy-graham.html.

About the Author

JERRY B. JENKINS is a widely published biographer and novelist (including the bestselling Left Behind series). Former vice president for publishing at the Moody Bible Institute, he also served on Moody's board of trustees for eighteen years, seven as chairman. His writing has appeared in *Time*, *Reader's Digest*, *Parade*, *Guideposts*, *Christianity Today*, and dozens of other periodicals. Twenty-one of his books have reached the *New York Times* Best Sellers List (seven in the number one spot). Jenkins spent thirteen months assisting Dr. Billy Graham with his autobiography, *Just As I Am*, which Jerry considers the privilege of a lifetime. He uses his website, www.JerryJenkins.com, to train writers.

Jerry and his wife, Dianna, have three grown sons and eight grandchildren.